knit along with

DEBBIE MACOMBER

A Turn in the Road

LEISURE ARTS, INC.
Little Rock, Arkansas

EDITORIAL STAFF
Editor-in-Chief: Susan White Sullivan
Director of Designer Relations: Cheryl Johnson
Special Projects Director: Susan Frantz Wiles
Senior Prepress Director: Mark Hawkins
Art Publications Director: Rhonda Shelby
Technical Editor: Cathy Hardy
Editorial Writer: Susan McManus Johnson
Art Category Manager: Lora Puls
Graphic Artists: Jacob Casleton
Senior Publications Designer: Dana Vaughn
Imaging Technician: Stephanie Johnson
Photography Manager: Katherine Laughlin
Contributing Photographers: Jason Masters
    and Ken West
Contributing Photostylists: Sondra Daniel
    and Cora Holdaway
Publishing Systems Administrator: Becky Riddle
Prepress Technician: Janie Marie Wright
Mac Information Technology Specialist: Robert Young

BUSINESS STAFF
President and Chief Executive Officer: Rick Barton
Vice President and Chief Operations Officer:
    Tom Siebenmorgen
Vice President of Sales: Mike Behar
Director of Finance and Administration:
    Laticia Mull Dittrich
National Sales Director: Martha Adams
Creative Services: Chaska Lucas
Information Technology Director: Hermine Linz
Controller: Francis Caple
Vice President, Operations: Jim Dittrich
Retail Customer Service Manager: Stan Raynor
Print Production Manager: Fred F. Pruss

ISBN-13: 978-1-60900-130-8

table of contents

debbie *Macomber*

Dear Friends,

In my newest Blossom Street book, *A Turn in the Road*, three Hamlin women from Seattle take a road trip together all the way to Vero Beach, Florida. Grandmother Ruth is anxious to arrive at her 50-year high school reunion. Mother Bethanne (Remember Bethanne from *A Good Yarn*?) is trying to decide if she can forget the past and reunite with her ex-husband. And daughter Annie is left reeling after the marriage proposal she expects turns into something quite different.

For each woman, the journey promises adventure and the exciting possibility of a new romance or a love rekindled. And of course, there's a little time to knit along the way!

Inspired by the story, the 18 portable designs in this pattern book are perfect for knitting thoughtful little gifts as you travel. I know I always have a future gift "on the needles" with me when I fly or drive—it's just so satisfying to turn those hours into something special for a loved one.

And really, isn't knitting all about showing others how much we care? That's why I've donated the proceeds from sales of my Leisure Arts Knit Along books to my favorite charities, including Warm Up America! and World Vision. On page 55, you'll find two blocks to knit for your own community charity efforts.

Wherever your travels take you, I'm so happy you've allowed me to share in your knitting adventures!

a word from
Leisure Arts
and Mira Books

Look for Debbie's heartwarming stories at bookstores everywhere, and collect all eleven of her knitting publications!

knit along with
DEBBIE MACOMBER

Read the books that inspired the projects.

Cedar Cove Series

Inspired by Debbie's popular Blossom Street and Cedar Cove book series, the Knit Along with Debbie Macomber companion books are a treasure trove of patterns to knit and crochet! And have you discovered the classic knit patterns in Debbie's Favorites or the thoughtful designs in Friendship Shawls and A Charity Guide for Knitters? Take time to indulge yourself with Debbie's heartwarming tales; then treat yourself to a world of creativity from Leisure Arts!

Item # 4658

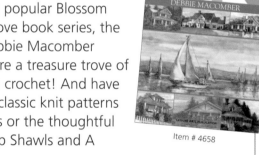

Blossom Street Series

Item # 5506

Item # 5121

Item # 4600

Item # 4729

Item # 4279

Item # 4135

Item # 4132

Other Debbie Macomber Publications

Item # 4692

Item # 4504

Item # 4803

4   www.leisurearts.com

You CAN take it with you ...your knitting, that is!

Like many knitters, Debbie Macomber often takes a project on the road with her. To suit the traveling theme of in *A Turn in the Road*, Debbie chose this collection of great take-along projects to knit.

What makes them perfect to pack for your trip? Either they are small projects, or they are easy to work! For example, the supplies for the Spa Cloth & Soap Sack or Accessory Clutch can be tucked into the corner of an overnight case. The Rainbow Flowers Baby Blanket is created panel-by-panel, so you can make one panel at a time. Once the beads are threaded, any piece of the Beaded Wedding Set can accompany you on your journey. Socks are always a great gift, and the pattern in this book is not only simple, it's sized for everyone. Even the Cowl doesn't need constant attention as you knit, because it's all Stockinette Stitch on circular needles between the basket weave design at the top and bottom.

Now you can comfortably knit all the way from Seattle, Washington to Vero Beach, Florida—or from your home to any destination of your choice! Why not look through these patterns and find your future gifts for birthdays, anniversaries, weddings, and Christmas? By the way, several of these heartfelt designs were made even more special with Debbie's beautiful Blossom Street™ Collection yarns.

Bethanne

"I think Dad wants to get back together." Bethanne's daughter, Annie, spoke with studied nonchalance. "He still loves you, Mom."

Bethanne's spoon hovered over her bowl of soup as they sat at a window table in their favorite café. Six years ago her world had imploded when her husband confessed that he'd fallen in love with another woman. With barely a backward glance, Grant had walked out. She'd heard his marriage to Tiffany had ended in divorce the previous year.

"Don't you have anything to say?" Annie asked. She watched her mother intently.

"Not really."

Annie, it seemed, had forgotten. But not Bethanne. At one time she had dreamed Grant would seek her forgiveness and come crawling back to her. But in the years since her own divorce, Bethanne had discovered a self she didn't know existed—a stronger, independent Bethanne.

This week, Grant had phoned and asked her to dinner. He wanted things back the way they used to be.

Dinner. She and Grant. After six years?

A Turn in the Road

Ruth

Bethanne glanced over at the French Café and saw her ex-mother-in-law, Ruth Hamlin, eating lunch. Despite the divorce, Bethanne had a warm relationship with Ruth. Bethanne rushed impulsively across the street.

"Ruth?"

Her mother-in-law looked up and broke into a smile. "Bethanne, my goodness. Robin suggested we meet for lunch. She never showed. But it doesn't really matter, because my daughter is not going to change my mind. She wants to talk me out of attending my fifty-year class reunion."

"I hope you go," Bethanne said.

"I am, and nothing she says will convince me otherwise." Bethanne had never seen Ruth so fired up. "And I intend to drive to Florida myself. That's all there is to it."

"Florida?" Bethanne repeated slowly. Her mother-in-law wanted to drive across the entire country? Alone?

Bethanne reached across the table and clasped Ruth's hand.

"I'll go with you," Bethanne said softly.

Annie

The phone rang, waking Bethanne from a sound sleep. Bethanne answered. "Hello?"

"Mom!" Annie wailed.

Shifting into a sitting position, Bethanne rubbed her eyes. "Annie, what's wrong?"

Annie tried to speak but Bethanne couldn't understand a word she said. What she did manage to grasp made no sense. "Vance is going away?" Bethanne asked.

"To Europe with Jessie."

This came out in a screech, which led Bethanne to believe Jessie was most likely a girl. So tonight's dinner at the Space Needle wasn't the marriage proposal Annie had so eagerly anticipated.

"Mom? Can I go to Florida with you and Grandma Hamlin? I can't bear to stay here alone."

"I'm sure your grandmother will be fine with it, and I'd love to have you."

This would be a fascinating trip across the country now that both her ex-mother-in-law and her daughter were coming. Well, interesting at any rate.

beaded wedding set

INTERMEDIATE

Finished Sizes

Bag: 7¹/₂" circumference x 5¹/₄" high (19 cm x 13.5 cm)
Garter: 1¹/₂" wide (4 cm) x desired length
Fingerless Gloves: 7¹/₂" circumference x 4³/₄" long (19 cm x 12 cm)
Veil: 9" (23 cm) diameter

MATERIALS

Super Fine Weight Yarn **SUPER FINE 1**
[2 ounces, 400 yards
(55 grams, 366 meters) per skein]:
   2 skeins
Straight knitting needles, size 2 (2.75 mm)
   or size needed for gauge
Set of 5 double pointed knitting needles,
   size 2 (2.75 mm) **or** size needed for gauge
#08 Seed Beads (silver lined crystal):
   Bag - 358
   Garter - 311 for 17" (43 cm) length *(see
      Size Note in Garter instructions, page 12)*
   Veil - 475
   Fingerless Gloves - 630
#06 Seed Beads (silver lined crystal) - 14 each for
   Bag and Gloves
Accent crystals - 2 each for Bag and Gloves
Heart crystals - 2 each for Bag and Gloves
Split-ring markers - 3
Stitch holder
Tapestry needle
Large eye beading needle
Tulle - 40" x 55" (101.5 cm x 139.5 cm)
³/₈" (10 mm) wide Ribbon - 2¹/₄ yards
   (2.057 meters) or desired length
Optional lining for Bag

GAUGE: In Stockinette Stitch,
   16 sts and 23 rows/rnds = 2"
   (5 cm)

Techniques used:
- M1 *(Figs. 9a & b, page 61)*
- YO *(Fig. 8a, page 60)*
- K2 tog *(Fig. 10, page 61)*
- P2 tog *(Fig. 15, page 62)*

When instructed to **slip a stitch**, always slip as if to **purl** with yarn held to **right** side. This allows the bead to be positioned on the right side of the piece, in front of the slipped stitch.

BAG
Thread a large eye beading needle with the yarn and string 358 #08 seed beads, adding extra beads just to make sure you have enough.

RUFFLE
Using straight needles, cast on 155 sts.

Row 1: K1, ★ WYB slip 1, slide bead up (next to needle), K1; repeat from ★ across.

Row 2 (Right side): (K1, P4) across.

Row 3: (K4, P1) across.

Row 4: ★ K1, P2, slide bead up, P2; repeat from ★ across.

Row 5: (K4, P1) across.

Row 6: (K1, P2 tog twice) across: 93 sts.

Row 7: (K2 tog, P1) across: 62 sts.

Row 8: K2, ★ WYF slip 1, slide bead up, K1; repeat from ★ across.

Row 9: Purl across.

Row 10 (Eyelet row): K1, (YO twice, K2 tog) across to last st, K1: 92 sts.

Row 11: P2, ★ purl into first YO letting second loop fall off needle, P1; repeat from ★ across: 62 sts.

BODY
Row 1: Knit across.

Row 2: P2, ★ WYB slip 1, slide bead up, P1; repeat from ★ across.

Row 3: Knit across.

Row 4: Purl across.

Row 5: K2, ★ WYF slip 1, slide bead up, K5; repeat from ★ across.

Row 6: Purl across.

Row 7: Knit across.

Row 8: Purl across.

Row 9: ★ K5, WYF slip 1, slide bead up; repeat from ★ across to last 2 sts, K2.

Row 10: Purl across.

Row 11: Knit across.

Row 12: Purl across.

Rows 13-44: Repeat Rows 5-12, 4 times.

Row 45: ★ K1, WYF slip 1, slide bead up; repeat from ★ across to last 2 sts, K2.

Row 46: Purl across.

Row 47: K2, ★ WYF slip 1, slide bead up, K1; repeat from ★ across.

Row 48: Purl across.

Row 49: ★ K1, WYF slip 1, slide bead up; repeat from ★ across to last 2 sts, K2.

BASE
Rows 1 and 2: Purl across.

Row 3 AND ALL WRONG SIDE ROWS THROUGH ROW 15: Knit across.

Row 4: (K7, K2 tog) across to last 8 sts, K8: 56 sts.

Row 6: (K6, K2 tog) across: 49 sts.

Row 8: (K5, K2 tog) across: 42 sts.

Row 10: (K4, K2 tog) across: 35 sts.

Row 12: (K3, K2 tog) across: 28 sts.

Row 14: (K2, K2 tog) across: 21 sts.

Row 16: (K1, K2 tog) across: 14 sts.

Row 17: K2 tog across: 7 sts.

Cut yarn leaving a long end for sewing.

FINISHING
Thread tapestry needle with end and slip remaining sts onto needle; gather tightly to close and secure end. Sew Base and side seam.

I-CORD TIE (Make 2)
Using double pointed needles, cast on 3 sts.

★ K3, slide sts to opposite end of needle; repeat from ★ until I-Cord measures approximately 13" (33 cm).

Bind off all sts in **knit**.

Weave one I-Cord Tie through Eyelet row; join ends. Beginning at opposite side, weave second I-Cord Tie through Eyelet row working through alternate spaces; join ends.

BEADED DECORATION (Make 2)
Using the diagram as a guide, string the beads in the following order: 4 #06 seed beads, accent bead, heart bead; then go back through the accent bead. String 3 more #06 seed beads, then go back through the first #06 seed bead.

DIAGRAM

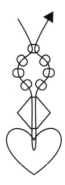

Attach a beaded decoration to joining on each I-Cord Tie.

Line bag if desired.

GARTER

Size Note: Garter instructions are for a 17" (43 cm) length. To adjust the length, add or subtract 10 sts to the cast on number for approximately every $^3/_4$" (2 cm) needed to be added or subtracted from the length. Adjust the number of beads, allowing approximately 11 beads for every 10 sts added or subtracted.

Thread a large eye beading needle with the yarn and string 311 #08 seed beads **or** number needed for desired length, adding extra beads just to make sure you have enough.

Using straight needles, cast on 285 sts.

Work Ruffle Rows 1-11 and Body Rows 1-4 same as Bag, page 10: 114 sts.

Bind off all sts in **knit**.

Weave 1 yard (.9144 meter) of ribbon **or** length needed through Eyelet row leaving ends long enough to tie in a bow.

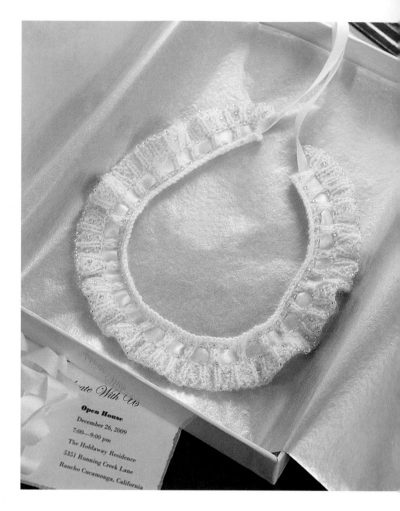

WEDDING VEIL

Thread a large eye beading needle with the yarn and string 475 #08 seed beads, adding extra beads just to make sure you have enough.

Using straight needles, cast on 215 sts.

Work Ruffle Rows 1-11 and Body Rows 1-21 same as Bag, page 10: 86 sts.

CROWN

Row 1: (P1, P2 tog) 3 times, purl across to last 9 sts, (P2 tog, P1) 3 times: 80 sts.

Row 2: (K8, K2 tog) across: 72 sts.

Row 3 AND ALL WRONG SIDE ROWS: ★ P1, WYB slip 1, slide bead up; repeat from ★ across to last 2 sts, P2.

Row 4: (K7, K2 tog) across: 64 sts.

Row 6: (K6, K2 tog) across: 56 sts.

Row 8: (K5, K2 tog) across: 48 sts.

Row 10: (K4, K2 tog) across: 40 sts.

Row 12: (K3, K2 tog) across: 32 sts.

Row 14: (K2, K2 tog) across: 24 sts.

Row 16: (K1, K2 tog) across: 16 sts.

Row 18: K2 tog across: 8 sts.

Row 19: Repeat Row 3.

Cut yarn leaving a long end for sewing.

FINISHING

Thread tapestry needle with end and slip remaining sts onto needle; gather to close (not tightly) and secure end; sew side seam.

VEIL

Cut an oval from the tulle, approximately 40" x 55" (101.5 cm x 139.5 cm). Using the diagram as a guide, sew a gathering stitch across the width, 5" (12.5 cm) from the top edge and gather to equal 3" (7.5 cm). Fold tulle along gathers and sew gathered edge to wrong side of knit cap centered at seam. Beginning at seam, weave 1¼ yards (1.143 meters) ribbon through Eyelet row; tie in a bow.

DIAGRAM

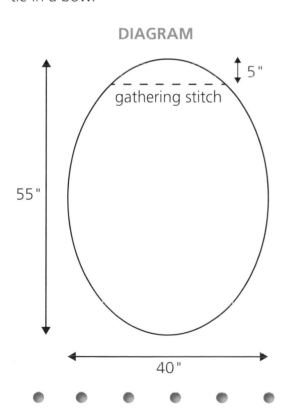

gathering stitch

5"

55"

40"

FINGERLESS GLOVES

Thread a large eye beading needle with the yarn and string 315 #08 seed beads, adding extra beads just to make sure you have enough.

RUFFLE
Using straight needles, cast on 140 sts.

Row 1: ★ K1, WYB slip 1, slide bead up (next to needle); repeat from ★ across to last 2 sts, K2.

Row 2 (Right side): (K1, P4) across.

Row 3: (K4, P1) across.

Row 4: ★ K1, P2, slide bead up, P2; repeat from ★ across.

Row 5: (K4, P1) across.

Row 6: (K1, P2 tog twice) across: 84 sts.

Row 7: (K2 tog, P1) across: 56 sts.

HAND
Slip 14 sts onto each of 4 double pointed needles *(Fig. 3c, page 58)*; place marker around first stitch to indicate beginning of rnd *(see Markers, page 57)*.

Rnd 1: With **wrong** side of Ruffle facing (right side of glove), (M1, knit across needle) 4 times: 60 sts.

Rnd 2: ★ K5, WYF slip 1, slide bead up; repeat from ★ around.

Rnds 3-5: Knit around.

Rnd 6: K2, WYF slip 1, slide bead up, ★ K5, WYF slip 1, slide bead up; repeat from ★ around to last 3 sts, K3.

Rnds 7-9: Knit around.

Rnds 10-18: Repeat Rnds 2-9 once, then repeat Rnd 2 once **more**.

GUSSET
Rnd 1 (Increase rnd): K 21, place marker, K1, M1, K3, M1, K1, place marker, knit across: 62 sts.

Rnd 2: Knit across to marker, P1, knit across to within one st of next marker, P1, knit across.

Rnd 3 (Increase rnd): Knit across to marker, P1, M1, knit across to within one st of next marker, M1, P1, knit across: 64 sts.

Rnd 4: K2, WYF slip 1, slide bead up, (K5, WYF slip 1, slide bead up) 3 times, P1, knit across to within one st of next marker, P1, WYF slip 1, slide bead up, (K5, WYF slip 1, slide bead up) 5 times, K3.

Rnds 5-7: Repeat Rnd 3, then repeat Rnds 2 and 3 once: 68 sts.

Rnd 8: (K5, WYF slip 1, slide bead up) 3 times, K3, P1, K5, WYF slip 1, slide bead up, K5, P1, K3, WYF slip 1, slide bead up, (K5, WYF slip 1, slide bead up) 5 times.

Rnds 9-19: Maintaining beading pattern, continue to increase 2 sts every other round in same manner, 6 times: 80 sts.

Rnd 20: Knit across in bead pattern to marker, remove marker, K1, slip next 23 sts onto st holder; **turn**, add on 3 sts *(Figs. 6a & b, page 59)*, **turn**, knit across in bead pattern removing marker: 60 sts.

Work even in beading pattern for 11 rnds or to desired length.

Beaded Bind Off: With **wrong** side facing, K1, ★ slide bead up, K1, pass first stitch on right needle over second st; repeat from ★ until one st remains on right needle; cut yarn and pull end through st.

THUMB

With **right** side facing, slip sts from st holder onto 2 double pointed needles; pick up 13 sts across Hand *(Fig. 18b, page 62)*; place marker around first st to indicate beginning of round: 36 sts.

Rnds 1-5: Knit around maintaining bead pattern.

Rnd 6: K2 tog, (K2, K2 tog) around to last st, K1: 26 sts.

Rnd 7: Knit around.

Rnd 8: K2, (K2 tog, K2) around: 20 sts.

Rnds 9-11: Knit around maintaining bead pattern.

Turn and work Beaded Bind Off.

FINISHING

Sew side seam on Ruffle.

BEADED DECORATION

Using the diagram on page 11 as a guide, string the beads in the following order: 4 #06 seed beads, accent bead, heart bead; then go back through the accent bead. String 3 more #06 seed beads, then go back through the first bead.

Using photo as a guide for placement, fold Ruffle toward Hand and sew beaded decoration in place, sewing through both layers. Be sure to have a right and a left glove.

Designs by Sandy Payne.

spiral socks

Size	Finished Foot Circumference	
X-Small	6"	(15 cm)
Small	7½"	(19 cm)
Medium	8½"	(21.5 cm)
Large	10"	(25.5 cm)

Size Note: Instructions are written for size X-Small with sizes Small, Medium, and Large in braces { }. Instructions will be easier to read if you circle all the numbers pertaining to your size. If only one number is given, it applies to all sizes.

MATERIALS

SUPER FINE
1

Super Fine Weight Yarn
[3.5 ounces, 462 yards
(100 grams, 420 meters) per skein]:
    1{1-1-2} skein(s)
Set of 5 double pointed knitting needles,
    size 2 (2.75 mm) **or** size needed for gauge
Split-ring marker
Stitch holders - 2
Tapestry needle

GAUGE: In Stockinette Stitch,
        32 sts and 44 rows/rnds = 4" (10 cm)

Techniques used:
• Increase *(Figs. 7a & b, page 59)*
• K2 tog *(Fig. 10, page 61)*
• SSK *(Figs. 12a-c, page 61)*
• P2 tog *(Fig. 15, page 62)*

RIBBING

Cast on 48{58-68-78} sts.

Divide sts between 4 double pointed needles *(Figs. 3a & c, page 58)*.

The yarn end indicates the beginning of the round.

Work in K1, P1 ribbing for 1" (2.5 cm).

LEG

The Leg begins with an increase to give you a multiple of 10 + 9 stitches. Because you have one less stitch than is needed for the pattern to come out even, a continuous spiral will form as you work. It is not necessary to mark the beginning of a round or to keep track of which round you are on.

Increase, P1, (K1, P1) twice, ★ K5, P1, (K1, P1) twice; repeat from ★ working in continuous rounds until Sock measures approximately $6^1/_2$ {$6^1/_2$-7-$7^1/_2$}"/16.5{16.5-18-19} cm from cast on edge **or** to desired length, ending by working a full repeat and leaving at least 5{3-5-3} sts at the end of the first needle, K5{3-5-3}: 49{59-69-79} sts.

It doesn't matter exactly where you end on the first needle. Ending the Leg as indicated will place the pattern so that the Seed Stitch section will run up each side of the top of the Foot after the Heel is completed.

HEEL FLAP

Dividing Stitches: Slip next 13{15-18-20} sts onto a st holder, slip next 12{14-17-19} sts onto a separate st holder for Instep to be worked later; **turn**.

When instructed to slip a stitch, always slip as if to **purl** with yarn held to **wrong** side.

With **wrong** side facing, work Row 1 across remaining sts onto one needle. The Heel Flap will be worked back and forth across these 24{30-34-40} sts.

Row 1: Slip 1, P1, (K1, P1) across.

Row 2: Slip 1, K1, (P1, K1) across.

Repeat Rows 1 and 2, 11{14-16-19} times, then repeat Row 1 once **more**.

TURN HEEL

Begin working in short rows as follows:

Row 1: Slip 1, K 14{18-20-24}, SSK, K1, leave remaining 6{8-10-12} sts unworked; **turn**.

Row 2: Slip 1, P 7{9-9-11}, P2 tog, P1, leave remaining 6{8-10-12} sts unworked; **turn**.

Row 3: Slip 1, K 8{10-10-12}, SSK, K1; turn.

Row 4: Slip 1, P 9{11-11-13}, P2 tog, P1; turn.

Work same as Rows 3 and 4, 2{3-4-5} times working one additional st before the decrease: 16{20-22-26} sts.

GUSSET

The remainder of the Sock will be worked in rounds.

Slip the Instep sts from the st holders onto separate needles.

FOUNDATION ROUND

With **right** side of Heel facing, using an empty needle and continuing with the working yarn, knit 8{10-11-13} of the Heel sts.
Place a split-ring marker around the next st to indicate the beginning of the round *(see Markers, page 57)*. Using an empty needle (this will be needle 1), knit across the remaining 8{10-11-13} Heel sts. With the same needle, pick up 12{15-17-20} sts along the side of the Heel Flap *(Fig. 18a, page 62)*.
With separate needles, work across the Instep sts (needles 2 and 3) as follows: K 1{3-1-3}, P1, K1, P1, (K7, P1, K1, P1) 2{2-3-3} times, K 1{3-1-3}.
With an empty needle, pick up 12{15-17-20} sts along the side of the Heel Flap. With the same needle, knit 8{10-11-13} Heel sts.

The stitch count is 20{25-28-33} sts on the first needle, 13{15-18-20} sts on the second needle, 12{14-17-19} sts on the third needle, and 20{25-28-33} sts on the fourth needle for a total of 65{79-91-105} sts.

GUSSET DECREASES

The pattern on the top of the Foot forms straight columns of Seed Stitch and Stockinette Stitch.

Rnd 1 (Decrease rnd)**:** Knit across to the last 3 sts on first needle, K2 tog, K1; work across the second and third needles as follows: K 0{2-0-2} *(see Zeros, page 57)*, P1, (K1, P1) twice, ★ K5, P1, (K1, P1) twice; repeat from ★ 1{1-2-2} time(s) **more**, K 0{2-0-2}; on fourth needle, K1, SSK, knit across: 63{77-89-103} sts.

Rnd 2: Knit across first needle; work across the second and third needles as follows: K1{3-1-3}, P1, K1, P1, ★ K7, P1, K1, P1; repeat from ★ 1{1-2-2} time(s) **more**, K1{3-1-3}; on fourth needle, knit across.

Repeat Rnds 1 and 2, 7{9-10-12} times: 49{59-69-79} sts.

FOOT

Work even until Foot measures approximately 5¼{8-8¾-9¾}"/13.5{20.5-22-25} cm from back of Heel **or** 1¼{1½-1¾-1¾}"/3{4-4.5-4.5} cm less than total desired finished length.

TOE

Rnd 1 (Decrease rnd)**:** Knit across first needle to last 3 sts, K2 tog, K1; on second needle, K1, SSK, knit across; on third needle, knit across to last 3 sts, K2 tog, K1; on fourth needle, K1, SSK, knit across: 45{55-65-75} sts.

Rnd 2: Knit around.

Repeat Rnds 1 and 2, 6{7-8-9} times: 21{27-33-39} sts.

Sizes X-Small and Medium Only: Using the fourth needle, knit across first needle; using an empty needle, K1, SSK, knit across remaining sts on second needle and third needle; cut yarn leaving a long end for grafting. There are 10{16} sts on both needles.

Sizes Small and Large Only: Using the fourth needle, knit across first needle to last 3 sts, K2 tog, K1; cut yarn leaving a long end for grafting. Slip the stitches from the third needle onto the second needle. There are 13{19} sts on both needles.

All Sizes: Graft the remaining sts together *(Figs. 20a & b, page 63)*.

Block Socks *(see Blocking, page 63)*.

Design by Cathy Hardy.

textured shawl

EASY +

Finished Size: 16½" x 60" (42 cm x 152.5 cm)

MATERIALS

Light Weight Yarn **LIGHT 3**
[1.75 ounces, 137 yards
(50 grams, 125 meters) per skein]:
  8 skeins
Straight knitting needles, sizes 7 (4.5 mm) **and**
  17 (12.75 mm) **or** sizes needed for gauge

GAUGE: With smaller size needles,
  in Garter Stitch (knit every row),
  20 sts = 4" (10 cm)

SHAWL

With smaller size needles, cast on 82 sts.

Rows 1-4: Knit across.

Row 5 (Right side)**:** With larger size needle, knit across.

Row 6: With smaller size needle, K1, ★ insert right needle through next 4 sts as if to **knit** *(Fig. 1)* and (K1, P1) twice all in same 4-st group; repeat from ★ across to last st, K1.

Fig. 1

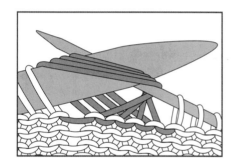

Rows 7-11: Knit across.

Row 12: K2, (P2, K2) across.

Row 13: Knit across.

Rows 14-34: Repeat Rows 12 and 13, 10 times, then repeat Row 12 once **more**.

Repeat Rows 1-34 for pattern until Shawl measures approximately 60" (152.5 cm) from cast on edge, ending by working Row 10.

Bind off all sts in **knit**.

Design by Cathy Hardy.

lace scarf

▣▣▢▢ EASY

Finished Size: 6" x 55" (15 cm x 139.5 cm)

MATERIALS

Fine Weight Yarn **[FINE 2]**
[3 ounces, 498 yards
(85 grams, 455 meters) per skein]:
  1 skein
Straight knitting needles, size 7 (4.5 mm)
  or size needed for gauge

GAUGE: In pattern, 20 sts = 3" (7.5 cm)
  (measured relaxed)

Gauge Swatch: 2³/₄" (7 cm) wide
Cast on 18 sts.
Row 1: K2, (P2, K2) across.
Row 2: P2, (K2 tog, YO, P2) across.
Row 3: K2, (P2, K2) across.
Row 4: P2, (K2, P2) across.
Row 5: K2, (P2, K2) across.
Row 6: P2, (YO, K2 tog, P2) across.
Row 7: K2, (P2, K2) across.
Row 8: P2, (K2, P2) across.
Rows 9-16: Repeat Rows 1-8.
Bind off all sts.

Techniques used:
- YO *(Figs. 8c & d, page 60)*
- K2 tog *(Fig. 10, page 61)*

STITCH GUIDE

FRONT CROSS (uses 2 sts)
Working in **front** of first st on left needle, knit into the second st making sure not to drop it off, then knit the first st letting both sts drop off the needle *(Figs. 4a & b, page 59)*.

SCARF

Cast on 40 sts.

Row 1: (K1, P1) across.

Row 2: (P1, K1) across.

Row 3: (K1, P1) across.

Row 4 (Right side)**:** P1, K1, P1, work Front Cross, P2, (K2 tog, YO, P2) across to last 5 sts, work Front Cross, K1, P1, K1.

Instructions continued on page 27.

spa cloth & soap sack

◖◗◻◻◻ EASY

Finished Sizes
Spa Cloth: 8"w x 8³/₄"h (20.5 cm x 22 cm)
Soap Sack: 6" circumference x 5³/₄" tall
(15 cm x 14.5 cm)

MATERIALS
100% Cotton Medium Weight Yarn **MEDIUM 4**
[1.75 ounces, 80 yards
(50 grams, 73 meters) per skein]:
   2 skeins
Straight knitting needles, size 7 (4.5 mm) **or**
   size needed for gauge
Yarn needle
¹/₈" (3 mm) wide Ribbon - 18" (45.5 cm) length

GAUGE: In Stockinette Stitch (knit one row,
   purl one row),
   17 sts and 26 rows = 4" (10 cm)

Techniques used:
• Increase *(Figs. 7a & b, page 59)*
• YO *(Figs. 8a & b, page 60)*
• K2 tog *(Fig. 10, page 61)*
• Slip 1 as if to **knit**, K2, PSSO *(Fig. 14, page 62)*

SPA CLOTH
Cast on 42 sts.

Row 1: Knit across.

Row 2 (Right side)**:** P2, (slip 1, K2, PSSO, P2)
across: 34 sts.

Row 3: K2, (P1, YO, P1, K2) across: 42 sts.

Row 4: P2, (K3, P2) across.

Row 5: K2, (P3, K2) across.

Rows 6-12: Repeat Rows 2-5 once, then repeat
Rows 2-4 once **more**.

Row 13: (K2, P3) twice, K 22, (P3, K2) twice.

Row 14: P2, (slip 1, K2, PSSO, P2) twice, K 18, P2,
(slip 1, K2, PSSO, P2) twice: 38 sts.

Row 15: (K2, P1, YO, P1) twice, K3, P 16, K3, (P1,
YO, P1, K2) twice: 42 sts.

Row 16: P2, (K3, P2) twice, K 18, P2, (K3, P2) twice.

Row 17: (K2, P3) twice, K3, P 16, K3, (P3, K2) twice.

Rows 18-44: Repeat Rows 14-17, 6 times; then repeat Rows 14-16 once **more**.

Row 45: (K2, P3) twice, K 22, (P3, K2) twice.

Rows 46-58: Repeat Rows 2-5, 3 times; then repeat Row 2 once **more**.

Bind off all sts in **knit**.

SOAP SACK
Cast on 16 sts.

Row 1 (Right side)**:** Increase in each st across: 32 sts.

Row 2: K2, (P3, K2) across.

Row 3: P2, (slip 1, K2, PSSO, P2) across: 26 sts.

Row 4: K2, (P1, YO, P1, K2) across: 32 sts.

Row 5: P2, (K3, P2) across.

Rows 6-30: Repeat Rows 2-5, 6 times; then repeat Row 2 once **more**.

Row 31 (Eyelet row)**:** K2, (YO, K2 tog) across to last 2 sts, K2.

Row 32: Purl across.

Row 33: Increase in each st across: 64 sts.

Row 34: Purl across.

Row 35: Knit across.

Row 36: Purl across.

Bind off all sts in **knit**, leaving a long end for sewing.

Weave seam *(Fig. 19, page 63)*, then weave yarn through cast on sts, gather tightly and secure end.

Weave ribbon through Eyelet row for drawstring.

Design by Rhonda White.

lace scarf   *Continued from page 22.*

Row 5: K1, P1, K1, (P2, K2) across to last 5 sts, P3, K1, P1.

Row 6: P1, K1, P1, (K2, P2) across to last 5 sts, K3, P1, K1.

Row 7: K1, P1, K1, (P2, K2) across to last 5 sts, P3, K1, P1.

Row 8: P1, K1, P1, work Front Cross, P2, (YO, K2 tog, P2) across to last 5 sts, work Front Cross, K1, P1, K1.

Row 9: K1, P1, K1, (P2, K2) across to last 5 sts, P3, K1, P1.

Row 10: P1, K1, P1, (K2, P2) across to last 5 sts, K3, P1, K1.

Row 11: K1, P1, K1, (P2, K2) across to last 5 sts, P3, K1, P1.

Row 12: P1, K1, P1, work Front Cross, P2, (K2 tog, YO, P2) across to last 5 sts, work Front Cross, K1, P1, K1.

Repeat Rows 5-12 for pattern until Scarf measures approximately 54¹⁄₂" (138.5 cm) from cast on edge or to desired length, ending by working Row 8 or Row 12.

Next Row: (K1, P1) across.

Next Row: (P1, K1) across.

Next Row: (K1, P1) across.

Bind off all sts in pattern.

Block Scarf for a lacy look *(see Blocking, page 63)*.

Design by Cathy Hardy.

baby bonnet & booties set

Finished Size: 6 months

MATERIALS

Super Fine Weight Yarn **SUPER FINE 1**
[1.75 ounces, 286 yards
(50 grams, 262 meters) per skein]:
Color A (Yellow) - 1 skein
Color B (White) - 1 skein
Straight knitting needles, sizes 2 (2.75 mm)
and 3 (3.25 mm) **or** sizes needed for gauge
Stitch holders - 2
Tapestry needle
Sewing needle and matching thread
³/₈" (10 mm) Ribbon - 1 yard (.9144 meter)

GAUGE: With larger size needles,
in Stockinette Stitch (knit one row,
purl one row),
28 sts and 36 rows = 4" (10 cm)

Techniques used:
- Increase *(Figs. 7a & b, page 59)*
- K2 tog *(Fig. 10, page 61)*
- P2 tog *(Fig. 15, page 62)*

BONNET
RIBBING

With smaller size needles and Color A, cast on
83 sts.

Row 1: K1, (P1, K1) across.

Row 2: P1, (K1, P1) across.

Repeat Rows 1 and 2 until Ribbing measures
approximately 1" (2.5 cm) from cast on edge,
ending by working Row 1.

CROWN

Carry yarn not being used loosely along the edge.

Change to larger size needles.

Row 1 (Right side)**:** With Color B, knit across.

Row 2: Purl across.

Rows 3 and 4: With Color A, knit across.

Repeat Rows 1-4 for pattern until piece measures
approximately 5" (12.5 cm) from cast on edge,
ending by working Row 4.

Cut Color A.

BACK

Row 1: With Color B, bind off 28 sts, knit across: 55 sts.

Row 2: Bind off 28 sts, purl across: 27 sts.

Work in Stockinette Stitch until Back measures approximately 4" (10 cm), ending by working a **knit** row.

Decrease Row: P2, P2 tog, (P1, P2 tog) 7 times, P2: 19 sts.

Slip remaining sts onto st holder; cut yarn.

FINISHING

Sew sides of Back to bound off edges of Crown.

NECK BAND

With **right** side facing, using smaller size needles and Color A, pick up 26 sts evenly spaced along end of rows on Ribbing and Crown *(Fig. 18a, page 62)*, slip 19 sts from Back st holder onto empty needle and knit across, pick up 26 sts evenly spaced along end of rows on Crown and Ribbing: 71 sts.

Row 1: P1, (K1, P1) across.

Row 2 (Right side)**:** K1, (P1, K1) across.

Repeat Rows 1 and 2 until Neck Band measures approximately 1" (2.5 cm), ending by working Row 1.

Bind off all sts in ribbing.

Using photo as a guide for placement, attach an 18" (45.5 cm) length of ribbon to each corner for ties.

BOOTIES

RIBBING

With smaller size needles and Color A, cast on 41 sts.

Row 1: K1, (P1, K1) across.

Row 2: P1, (K1, P1) across.

Repeat Rows 1 and 2 until Ribbing measures approximately 1½" (4 cm) from cast on edge, ending by working Row 1.

INSTEP

Change to larger size needles.

Row 1 (Right side)**:** K 15, slip sts just worked onto st holder, K1, increase, K7, increase, K1, slip remaining 15 sts onto second st holder: 13 sts.

Row 2: Knit across.

Carry yarn not being used loosely along the edge.

Row 3: With Color B, knit across.

Row 4: Purl across.

Rows 5 and 6: With Color A, knit across.

Rows 7-16: Repeat Rows 3-6 twice, then repeat Rows 3 and 4 once **more**.

Cut both colors.

SIDES

With **right** side facing, slip 15 sts from first st holder onto empty needle, with Color A, pick up 8 sts evenly spaced along end of rows on Instep *(Fig. 18a, page 62)*, knit across Instep, pick up 8 sts evenly spaced along end of rows on Instep, slip 15 sts from st holder onto empty needle and knit across: 59 sts.

Row 1: Knit across.

Row 2: With Color B, knit across.

Row 3: Purl across.

Rows 4 and 5: With Color A, knit across.

Row 6: With Color B, knit across.

Row 7: P 23, P2 tog, (P3, P2 tog) twice, purl across; cut Color B: 56 sts.

Rows 8 and 9: With Color A, knit across.

SOLE

Work in short rows as follows:

Row 1: K 32, K2 tog, leave remaining 22 sts unworked; **turn.**

Rows 2-35: K9, K2 tog, leave remaining sts unworked; **turn.**

Row 36: K9, K2 tog, K5: 20 sts.

Bind off all sts in **knit.**

Weave back seam *(Fig. 19, page 63).*
Sew back of Sole to Sides.

Design by Carole Prior.

rainbow flowers baby blanket

INTERMEDIATE

Finished Size: 30½" x 41" (77.5 x 104 cm)

MATERIALS

SUPER FINE 1

Super Fine Weight Yarn
[1.75 ounces, 286 yards
(50 grams, 262 meters) per skein]:
  White - 2 skeins
  Blue - 1 skein
  Purple - 1 skein
  Yellow - 1 skein
  Pink - 1 skein
Straight knitting needles, size 3 (3.25 mm) **or**
  size needed for gauge
Tapestry needle
T-pins

GAUGE: In Stockinette Stitch,
          28 sts and 36 rows = 4" (10 cm)

Techniques used:
- YO *(Figs. 8a & b, page 60)*
- K2 tog *(Fig. 10, page 61)*
- K3 tog *(Fig. 11, page 61)*
- Slip 1 as if to **knit**, K1, PSSO *(Figs. 13a & b, page 61)*
- P2 tog *(Fig. 15, page 62)*

DIAMOND PANEL (Make 3)

With White, cast on 17 sts.

Row 1 (Right side)**:** K1, purl across to last st, K1.

Row 2: Purl across.

Rows 3-6: Repeat Rows 1 and 2 twice.

Row 7: K1, (P1, YO, P2 tog) across to last st, K1.

Row 8 AND ALL WRONG SIDE ROWS: Purl across.

Row 9: Knit across.

Row 11: K7, slip 1, K1, PSSO, YO, K8.

Row 13: K6, slip 1, K1, PSSO, YO, K1, YO, K2 tog, K6.

Row 15: K5, slip 1, K1, PSSO, YO, K3, YO, K2 tog, K5.

Row 17: K4, slip 1, K1, PSSO, YO, K5, YO, K2 tog, K4.

Row 19: K6, YO, K2 tog, K1, slip 1, K1, PSSO, YO, K6.

Row 21: K7, YO, K3 tog, YO, K7.

Row 23: K7, K2 tog, YO, K8.

Rows 25, 27, and 29: Knit across.

Rows 31-366: Repeat Rows 11-30, 16 times; then repeat Rows 11-26 once **more**.

Row 367: K1, (P1, YO, P2 tog) across to last st, K1.

Row 368: Purl across.

Row 369: K1, purl across to last st, K1.

Rows 370-372: Repeat Rows 368 and 369 once, then repeat Row 368 once **more**.

Bind off all sts in **purl**.

RIGHT DIAMOND PANEL
With White, cast on 20 sts.

Row 1 (Right side)**:** Purl across to last st, K1.

Row 2: Purl across.

Rows 3-6: Repeat Rows 1 and 2 twice.

Row 7: P5, YO, P2 tog, (P1, YO, P2 tog) across to last st, K1.

Row 8 AND ALL WRONG SIDE ROWS: Purl across.

Row 9: P3, knit across.

Row 11: P3, K7, slip 1, K1, PSSO, YO, K8.

Row 13: P3, K6, slip 1, K1, PSSO, YO, K1, YO, K2 tog, K6.

Row 15: P3, K5, slip 1, K1, PSSO, YO, K3, YO, K2 tog, K5.

Row 17: P3, K4, slip 1, K1, PSSO, YO, K5, YO, K2 tog, K4.

Row 19: P3, K6, YO, K2 tog, K1, slip 1, K1, PSSO, YO, K6.

Row 21: P3, K7, YO, K3 tog, YO, K7.

Row 23: P3, K7, K2 tog, YO, K8.

Rows 25, 27, and 29: P3, knit across.

Rows 31-366: Repeat Rows 11-30, 16 times; then repeat Rows 11-26 once **more**.

Row 367: P5, YO, P2 tog, (P1, YO, P2 tog) across to last st, K1.

Row 368: Purl across.

Row 369: Purl across to last st, K1.

Rows 370-372: Repeat Rows 368 and 369 once, then repeat Row 368 once **more**.

Bind off all sts in **purl**.

LEFT DIAMOND PANEL
With White, cast on 20 sts.

Row 1 (Right side)**:** K1, purl across.

Row 2: Purl across.

Rows 3-6: Repeat Rows 1 and 2 twice.

Row 7: K1, (P1, YO, P2 tog) across to last 4 sts, P4.

Row 8 AND ALL WRONG SIDE ROWS: Purl across.

Row 9: Knit across to last 3 sts, P3.

Row 11: K7, slip 1, K1, PSSO, YO, K8, P3.

Row 13: K6, slip 1, K1, PSSO, YO, K1, YO, K2 tog, K6, P3.

Row 15: K5, slip 1, K1, PSSO, YO, K3, YO, K2 tog, K5, P3.

Row 17: K4, slip 1, K1, PSSO, YO, K5, YO, K2 tog, K4, P3.

Row 19: K6, YO, K2 tog, K1, slip 1, K1, PSSO, YO, K6, P3.

Row 21: K7, YO, K3 tog, YO, K7, P3.

Row 23: K7, K2 tog, YO, K8, P3.

Rows 25, 27, and 29: Knit across to last 3 sts, P3.

Rows 31-366: Repeat Rows 11-30, 16 times; then repeat Rows 11-26 once **more**.

Row 367: K1, (P1, YO, P2 tog) across to last 4 sts, P4.

Row 368: Purl across.

Row 369: K1, purl across.

Rows 370-372: Repeat Rows 368 and 369 once, then repeat Row 368 once **more**.

Bind off all sts in **purl**.

FLOWER PANELS (Make 4)
With White, cast on 35 sts.

Row 1 (Right side)**:** K1, purl across to last st, K1.

Row 2: Purl across.

Rows 3-6: Repeat Rows 1 and 2 twice.

Row 7: K1, (P1, YO, P2 tog) across to last st, K1.

Row 8 AND ALL WRONG SIDE ROWS: Purl across.

Row 9: Knit across.

Row 11: K 16, slip 1, K1, PSSO, YO, K 17.

Row 13: K 15, slip 1, K1, PSSO, YO, K1, YO, K2 tog, K 15.

Row 15: K 14, slip 1, K1, PSSO, YO, K3, YO, K2 tog, K 14.

Row 17: K 13, slip 1, K1, PSSO, YO, K5, YO, K2 tog, K 13.

Row 19: K 15, YO, K2 tog, K1, slip 1, K1, PSSO, YO, K 15.

Row 21: K 16, YO, K3 tog, YO, K 16.

Row 23: K 16, K2 tog, YO, K 17.

Row 25: Knit across.

On the next right side row, begin using one of the other four colors. Rows 27-346 of each Flower Panel will be worked with either Blue, Purple, Yellow, or Pink.

Row 27: Cut White; with one of the colors, knit across.

Row 29: Knit across.

Row 31: K 15, slip 1, K1, PSSO, YO, K1, YO, K2 tog, K 15.

Row 33: K 12, slip 1, K1, PSSO, YO, K1, YO, K2 tog, K1, slip 1, K1, PSSO, YO, K1, YO, K2 tog, K 12.

Row 35: K 11, slip 1, K1, PSSO, YO, K2, YO, K2 tog, K1, slip 1, K1, PSSO, YO, K2, YO, K2 tog, K 11.

Instructions continued on page 39.

balls

Approximate Finished Sizes
Small: 2" (5 cm) diameter
Medium: 3" (7.5 cm) diameter

MATERIALS
100% Cotton Medium Weight Yarn
[2-2.5 ounces, 95-120 yards
(56-71 grams, 86-109 meters) per skein]:
    1 skein *(see yarn note)*
Straight knitting needles, size 8 (5 mm)
Polyester fiberfill for a soft ball **or** plastic
    pellets and one knee high stocking for a
    heavier ball
Yarn needle

Yarn Note: You can use solid or variegated yarn, or a combination of many colors to form stripes. One skein will make 4 or 5 medium balls or 10 to 12 small balls.

These balls are very versatile. When stuffed with soft filling, they are great for babies, children, and even dogs to play with. The balls can be filled with plastic pellets that are contained in a stocking, turning them into wonderful juggling balls. The small sized ball also makes a great hacky sack.

Note: Gauge is not of great importance. Your balls can be slightly larger or smaller.

Techniques used:
- Increase *(Figs. 7a & b, page 59)*
- K2 tog *(Fig. 10, page 61)*

SMALL BALL
Cast on 9 sts.

Row 1 (Right side): Increase in each st across: 18 sts.

Row 2: Purl each st across.

Row 3: Knit each st across.

Row 4: Purl each st across.

Rows 5-8: Knit each st across.

Rows 9-13: Repeat Rows 4-8.

Rows 14-16: Repeat Rows 2-4.

Row 17: K2 tog across: 9 sts.

Cut the yarn leaving a long end for sewing.

MEDIUM BALL

Our striped Ball was worked in the following stripe sequence: 6 rows Green, 2 rows Blue, 6 rows Variegated, 2 rows Blue, and 7 rows Green.

Cast on 9 sts.

Row 1 (Right side): Increase in each st across: 18 sts.

Row 2: Purl each st across.

Row 3: Increase in each st across: 36 sts.

Row 4: Purl each st across.

Row 5: Knit each st across.

Row 6: Purl each st across.

Rows 7-10: Knit each st across.

Rows 11-20: Repeat Rows 4-10 once, then repeat Rows 4-6 once **more**.

Row 21: K2 tog across: 18 sts.

Row 22: Purl each st across.

Row 23: K2 tog across: 9 sts.

Cut the yarn(s) leaving a long end for sewing.

FINISHING

Thread a yarn needle with the long end and slip the 9 sts from the knitting needle onto the yarn needle. Pull the yarn to gather the stitches tightly and close the hole, then make a knot to secure the yarn. Weave the seam halfway closed *(Fig. 19, page 63)*; do not remove the yarn needle or cut the yarn.

SOFT BALL

Stuff the Ball with fiberfill then finish weaving the seam using more fiberfill as needed; secure the yarn but do **not** cut.

HEAVIER BALL

Pour approximately 1/4 cup of plastic pellets for the Small Ball and 2/3 cup of plastic pellets for the Medium Ball into the toe of a knee high stocking. Use the Ball as guide to see if you'd like more or less pellets. Twist the stocking to close and pull the unused part over the plastic pellets ball. Repeat as many times as needed to make the pellets secure, then either knot the remaining part or sew the top closed.

Place the pellet ball inside the knit Ball and finish weaving the seam; secure the yarn but do **not** cut.

ALL BALLS

Weave the yarn end through the beginning 9 sts; pull the yarn to gather the stitches tightly and close the hole, then make a knot to secure the yarn. Insert the yarn needle into the Ball and push it out to the other side. Cut the yarn end close to the Ball.

Design by Kay Meadors.

rainbow flowers baby blanket *Continued from page 35.*

Row 37: K 10, slip 1, K1, PSSO, YO, K3, YO, K2 tog, K1, slip 1, K1 PSSO, YO, K3, YO, K2 tog, K 10.

Row 39: K9, slip 1, K1, PSSO, YO, K4, YO, K2 tog, K1, slip 1, K1, PSSO, YO, K4, YO, K2 tog, K9.

Row 41: K8, slip 1, K1, PSSO, YO, K5, YO, K2 tog, K1, slip 1, K1, PSSO, YO, K5, YO, K2 tog, K8.

Row 43: K9, YO, K2 tog, K2, (slip 1, K1, PSSO, YO) twice, K1, (YO, K2 tog) twice, K2, slip 1, K1, PSSO, YO, K9.

Row 45: K9, YO, K2 tog, K1, (slip 1, K1, PSSO, YO) twice, K3, (YO, K2 tog) twice, K1, slip 1, K1, PSSO, YO, K9.

Row 47: K9, YO, K2 tog, (slip 1, K1, PSSO, YO) twice, K5, (YO, K2 tog) twice, slip 1, K1, PSSO, YO, K9.

Row 49: K9, YO, K3 tog, YO, slip 1, K1, PSSO, YO, K7, YO, K2 tog, YO, K3 tog, YO, K9.

Row 51: K 11, slip 1, K1, PSSO, YO, K3, slip 1, K1, PSSO, YO, K4, YO, K2 tog, K 11.

Row 53: K 10, slip 1, K1, PSSO, YO, K3, slip 1, K1, PSSO, YO, K1, YO, K2 tog, K3, YO, K2 tog, K 10.

Row 55: K9, slip 1, K1, PSSO, YO, K3, slip 1, K1, PSSO, YO, (K3, YO, K2 tog) twice, K9.

Row 57: K 13, slip 1, K1, PSSO, YO, K5, YO, K2 tog, K 13.

Row 59: K 15, YO, K2 tog, K1, slip 1, K1, PSSO, YO, K 15.

Row 61: K 16, YO, K3 tog, YO, K 16.

Row 63: K 16, K2 tog, YO, K 17.

Rows 65, 67, and 69: Knit across.

Rows 71-346: Repeat Rows 31-70, 6 times; then repeat Rows 31-66 once **more**.

Row 347: Cut yarn; with White, knit across.

Rows 348-366: Repeat Rows 8-26.

Row 367: K1, (P1, YO, P2 tog) across to last st, K1.

Rows 368: Purl across.

Row 369: K1, purl across to last st, K1.

Rows 370-372: Repeat Rows 368 and 369 once, then repeat Row 368 once **more**.

Bind off all sts in **purl**.

Block Panels *(see Blocking, page 63)*.

Pin two Panels together side-by-side and matching diamonds, then weave seams *(Fig. 19, page 63)*, joining Panels in the following order from right to left: Right Diamond Panel, Pink Flower Panel, Diamond Panel, Yellow Flower Panel, Diamond Panel, Purple Flower Panel, Diamond Panel, Blue Flower Panel, Left Diamond Panel.

Design by Cathy Hardy.

cable hat & mittens

Sizes: Child{Adult}
Finished Sizes
  Hat: 14 1/2{17 1/2}"/37{44.5} cm circumference
  Mittens: 6 3/4{8 1/2}"/17{21.5} cm circumference

Size Note: Instructions are written for Child size with Adult size in braces { }. Instructions will be easier to read if you circle all the numbers pertaining to your size. If only one number is given, it applies to both sizes.

MATERIALS
  Medium Weight Yarn ⑷
  [1.75 ounces, 93 yards
  (50 grams, 85 meters) per skein]:
    3{4} skeins
  Straight knitting needles, sizes 7 (4.5 mm)
    and 9 (5.5 mm) **or** sizes needed for gauge
  Markers - 4
  Cable needle
  Stitch holders - 2
  Yarn needle

GAUGE: With larger size needles,
    in Seed Stitch,
    20 sts and 28 rows = 4" (10 cm)

Gauge Swatch: 2" (5 cm) square
With larger size needles, cast on 10 sts.
Row 1: (K1, P1) across.
Row 2: (P1, K1) across.
Rows 3-14: Repeat Rows 1 and 2, 6 times.
Bind off all sts.

Techniques used:
• Increase *(Figs. 7a & b, page 59)*
• K2 tog *(Fig. 10, page 61)*
• P2 tog *(Fig. 15, page 62)*
• P3 tog *(Fig. 16, page 62)*

STITCH GUIDE
CABLE (uses 6 sts)
Slip 3 sts onto cable needle and hold in **back** of work, K3 from left needle, K3 from cable needle.

HAT
RIBBING
With smaller size needles, cast on 82{98} sts.

Child Size Only
Row 1: K2, (P2, K2) across.

Row 2: P2, (K2, P2) across.

Adult Size Only
Row 1: P2, (K2, P2) across.

Row 2: K2, (P2, K2) across.

Both Sizes
Rows 3-6: Repeat Rows 1 and 2 twice.

BODY
Change to larger size needles.

Row 1 (Right side)**:** K2, ★ (P1, K1) 2{3} times, P2, K6, P2, (K1, P1) 2{3} times, K2; repeat from ★ across.

Row 2: P3, ★ † K1, (P1, K1) 2{3} times, P6, K1, (P1, K1) 2{3} times †, P4; repeat from ★ 2 times **more**, then repeat from † to † once, P3.

Rows 3 and 4: Repeat Rows 1 and 2.

Row 5: K2, ★ (P1, K1) 2{3} times, P2, work Cable, P2, (K1, P1) 2{3} times, K2; repeat from ★ across.

Rows 6-12: Repeat Row 2, then repeat Rows 1 and 2, 3 times.

Repeat Rows 5-12 for pattern until Hat measures approximately 5½{6}"/14{15} cm from cast on edge, ending by working a **wrong** side row.

CROWN
Row 1 (Decrease row)**:** K2, ★ P3 tog, work across 12{16} sts in pattern, P3 tog, place marker *(see Markers, page 57)*, K2; repeat from ★ across: 66{82} sts.

Row 2: Work across in pattern.

Row 3 (Decrease row)**:** K2, ★ P3 tog, work across in pattern to within 3 sts of next marker, P3 tog, K2; repeat from ★ across: 50{66} sts.

Child Size Only - Row 4: Work across in pattern removing markers.

Adult Size Only - Rows 4-6: Repeat Rows 2 and 3 once, then repeat Row 2 once **more** removing markers: 50 sts.

Both Sizes
Row 5{7}: (K5, K2 tog) across to last st, K1: 43 sts.

Row 6{8}: Purl across.

Row 7{9}: (K4, K2 tog) across to last st, K1: 36 sts.

Row 8{10}: Purl across.

Row 9{11}: (K3, K2 tog) across to last st, K1: 29 sts.

Row 10{12}: Purl across.

Row 11{13}: (K2, K2 tog) across to last st, K1: 22 sts.

Row 12{14}: Purl across.

Row 13{15}: K1, (K2 tog, K1) across: 15 sts.

Row 14{16}: P1, P2 tog across; cut yarn leaving a long end for sewing: 8 sts.

Thread yarn needle with end and slip remaining sts onto yarn needle; gather tightly and secure end; weave seam *(Fig. 19, page 63)*.

LEFT MITTEN
RIBBING
With smaller size needles, cast on 38{46} sts.

Row 1: K3{1}, (P2, K2) across to last 3{1} st(s), P3{1}.

Repeat Row 1 until Ribbing measures approximately 2¹⁄₂{3}"/6.5{7.5} cm from cast on edge.

THUMB GUSSET
Change to larger size needles.

Row 1 (Right side)**:** K 19{23}, place marker *(see Markers, page 57)*, (P1, K1) 2{3} times, P2, K6, P2, K1, (P1, K1) 2{3} times.

Row 2 AND ALL WRONG SIDE ROWS: K1, (P1, K1) 3{4} times, P6, K1, (P1, K1) 2{3} times, purl across.

Row 3: Knit across to marker, (P1, K1) 2{3} times, P2, K6, P2, K1, (P1, K1) 2{3} times.

Row 5 (Increase row)**:** Knit across to within 2 sts of marker, place marker, increase twice, (P1, K1) 2{3} times, P2, work Cable, P2, K1, (P1, K1) 2{3} times: 40{48} sts.

Row 7 (Increase row)**:** Knit across to first marker, increase, knit across to within one st of next marker, increase, (P1, K1) 2{3} times, P2, K6, P2, K1, (P1, K1) 2{3} times: 42{50} sts.

Row 9: Repeat Row 7: 44{52} sts.

Row 11: Repeat Row 7: 46{54} sts.

Adult Size Only - Row 13: Knit across to first marker, increase, knit across to within one st of next marker, increase, (P1, K1) 3 times, P2, work Cable, P2, K1, (P1, K1) 3 times: 56 sts.

Both Sizes - Row 13{15}: Knit across to first marker, remove marker, slip sts just worked onto st holder, knit across to marker, remove marker, slip remaining 19{23} sts onto second st holder: 10{12} sts.

THUMB
Beginning with a purl row, work in Stockinette Stitch (purl one row, knit one row) until Thumb measures approximately 2{2¹⁄₂}"/5{6.5} cm **or** to desired length, ending by working a **purl** row.

Last Row: K2 tog across; cut yarn leaving a long end for sewing: 5{6} sts.

Thread yarn needle with end and slip remaining sts onto yarn needle; gather tightly and secure end; weave seam *(Fig. 19, page 63)*.

HAND

Child Size Only - Row 1: With **right** side facing, slip 19 sts from second st holder onto larger size needle; (P1, K1) twice, P2, work Cable, P2, K1, (P1, K1) twice.

Adult Size Only - Row 1: With **right** side facing, slip 23 sts from second st holder onto larger size needle; (P1, K1) 3 times, P2, K6, P2, K1, (P1, K1) 3 times.

Both Sizes - Row 2: K1, (P1, K1) 3{4} times, P6, (K1, P1) 3{4} times; slip sts from st holder onto empty needle and purl across: 36{44} sts.

Work in pattern, working Cable every eighth row, until piece measures approximately 5½{6½}"/14{16.5} cm from top of Ribbing **or** 1" (2.5 cm) less than desired finished length, ending by working a **wrong** side row.

SHAPING

Row 1: (K2, K2 tog) across: 27{33} sts.

Row 2: Purl across.

Row 3: (K2, K2 tog) across to last 3{1} st(s), K3{1}: 21{25} sts.

Row 4: Purl across.

Row 5: (K2, K2 tog) across to last st, K1: 16{19} sts.

Row 6: Purl across.

Row 7: K2 tog across to last 0{1} st(s) *(see Zeros, page 57)*, K 0{1}: 8{10} sts.

Row 8: Purl across; cut yarn leaving a long end for sewing.

Thread yarn needle with end and slip remaining sts onto yarn needle; gather tightly and secure end; weave seam.

RIGHT MITTEN
RIBBING

With smaller size needles, cast on 38{46} sts.

Row 1: P3{1}, (K2, P2) across to last 3{1} st(s), K3{1}.

Repeat Row 1 until Ribbing measures approximately 2½{3}"/6.5{7.5} cm from cast on edge.

THUMB GUSSET

Change to larger size needles.

Row 1 (Right side)**:** K1, (P1, K1) 2{3} times, P2, K6, P2, (K1, P1) 2{3} times, place marker, knit across.

Row 2: Purl across to marker, (P1, K1) 3{4} times, P6, K1, (P1, K1) 3{4} times.

Row 3: K1, (P1, K1) 2{3} times, P2, K6, P2, (K1, P1) 2{3} times, knit across.

Row 4: Repeat Row 2.

Row 5 (Increase row)**:** K1, (P1, K1) 2{3} times, P2, work Cable, P2, (K1, P1) 2{3} times, increase twice, place marker, knit across: 40{48} sts.

Row 6 AND ALL WRONG SIDE ROWS: Purl across to second marker, (P1, K1) 3{4} times, P6, K1, (P1, K1) 3{4} times.

Row 7 (Increase row): K1, (P1, K1) 2{3} times, P2, K6, P2, (K1, P1) 2{3} times, increase, knit across to within one st of next marker, increase, knit across: 42{50} sts.

Row 9: Repeat Row 7: 44{52} sts.

Row 11: Repeat Row 7: 46{54} sts.

Child Size Only - Row 13: K1, (P1, K1) twice, P2, work Cable, P2, (K1, P1) twice, remove marker, slip sts just worked onto st holder, knit across to marker, remove marker, slip remaining 17 sts onto second st holder: 10 sts.

Adult Size Only
Row 13: K1, (P1, K1) 3 times, P2, work Cable, P2, (K1, P1) 3 times, increase, knit across to within one st of next marker, increase, knit across: 56 sts.

Row 15: K1, (P1, K1) 3 times, P2, K6, P2, (K1, P1) 3 times, remove marker, slip sts just worked onto st holder, knit across to marker, remove marker, slip remaining 21 sts onto second st holder: 12 sts.

THUMB
Beginning with a purl row, work in Stockinette Stitch until Thumb measures same as Left Mitten, ending by working a **purl** row.

Last Row: K2 tog across; cut yarn leaving a long end for sewing: 5{6} sts.

Thread yarn needle with end and slip remaining sts onto yarn needle; gather tightly and secure end; weave seam.

HAND
Row 1: With **right** side facing, slip sts from second st holder onto larger size needle and knit across: 17{21} sts.

Row 2: Purl across; slip sts from st holder onto empty needle, (P1, K1) 3{4} times, P6, K1, (P1, K1) 3{4} times: 36{44} sts.

Work in pattern, working Cable every eighth row, until piece measures same as Left Mitten, ending by working a **wrong** side row.

SHAPING
Work same as Left Mitten.

Design by Reba Beard King.

cowl

Finished Size: 13" high x 26" circumference
(33 cm x 66 cm)

MATERIALS

LIGHT 3

Light Weight Yarn
[3.5 ounces, 253 yards
(100 grams, 230 meters) per skein]:
  1 skein
24" (61 cm) Circular knitting needle, size
  6 (4 mm) **or** size needed for gauge
Marker

GAUGE: In Stockinette Stitch,
21 sts and 27 rnds/rows = 4" (10 cm)

BOTTOM BORDER

Cast on 136 sts *(see Using A Circular Needle, page 58)*; place marker to indicate the beginning of the round *(see Markers, page 57)*.

Rnds 1-4: ★ K4, P4; repeat from ★ around.

Rnds 5-8: ★ P4, K4; repeat from ★ around.

BODY

Remove marker and knit around for Stockinette Stitch until piece measures approximately 12" (30.5 cm) from cast on edge **or** 1" (2.5 cm) less than desired height.

TOP BORDER

Rnds 1-8: Place marker and work same as Bottom Border.

Bind off all sts in pattern.

Design by Cathy Hardy.

cable slippers

◨◧▢▢ EASY +

Size	Finished Foot Circumference		Finished Length	
Small	8"	(20.5 cm)	9"	(23 cm)
Medium	8³/₄"	(22 cm)	10"	(25.5 cm)
Large	9¹/₄"	(23.5 cm)	11"	(28 cm)

Size Note: Instructions are written for size Small with sizes Medium and Large in braces { }. Instructions will be easier to read if you circle all the numbers pertaining to your size. If only one number is given, it applies to all sizes.

MATERIALS

Medium Weight Yarn

MEDIUM 4

[4 ounces, 203 yards (113 grams, 186 meters) per skein]:
   2 skeins
Straight knitting needles, sizes 8 (5 mm) **and** 10 (6 mm) **or** sizes needed for gauge
Cable needle
Stitch holder
Yarn needle

Slippers are made holding 2 strands of yarn together throughout.

GAUGE: With larger size needles, in Seed Stitch, 12 sts and 20 rows = 4" (10 cm)

Gauge Swatch: 4" (10 cm) square
With larger size needles, cast on 12 sts.
Row 1: (K1, P1) across.
Row 2: (P1, K1) across.
Rows 3-20: Repeat Rows 1 and 2, 9 times.
Bind off all sts.

Techniques used:

* Increase *(Figs. 7a & b, page 59)*
* M1 *(Figs. 9a & b, page 61)*
* K2 tog *(Fig. 10, page 61)*
* Slip 1 as if to **knit**, K1, PSSO *(Figs. 13a & b, page 61)*
* P2 tog *(Fig. 15, page 62)*

STITCH GUIDE ··················

BACK CABLE (uses 4 sts)
Slip next 2 sts onto cable needle and hold in **back** of work, K2 from left needle, K2 from cable needle.
FRONT CABLE (uses 4 sts)
Slip next 2 sts onto cable needle and hold in **front** of work, K2 from left needle, K2 from cable needle.
BACK TWIST (uses 4 sts)
Slip next 2 sts onto cable needle and hold in **back** of work, K2 from left needle, P2 from cable needle.
FRONT TWIST (uses 4 sts)
Slip next 2 sts onto cable needle and hold in **front** of work, P2 from left needle, K2 from cable needle.

TOP

FIRST SIDE

With larger size needles, cast on 11 sts.

Row 1: P1, K2, P4, K3, P1.

Row 2 (Right side): K1, P3, K4, P2, K1.

Row 3: P1, K2, P4, K3, P1.

Row 4: K1, P3, work Back Cable, P2, K1.

Repeat Rows 1-4 for pattern until First Side measures approximately 4$\frac{1}{2}${5$\frac{1}{2}$-6$\frac{1}{2}$}"/ 11.5{14-16.5} cm from cast on edge, ending by working Row 4.

Slip sts onto st holder; cut yarn.

SECOND SIDE

With larger size needles, cast on 11 sts.

Row 1: P1, K3, P4, K2, P1.

Row 2 (Right side): K1, P2, K4, P3, K1.

Row 3: P1, K3, P4, K2, P1.

Row 4: K1, P2, work Front Cable, P3, K1.

Repeat Rows 1-4 for pattern until Second Side measures same as First Side, ending by working Row 4.

INSTEP

Row 1 (Joining row): P1, K3, P4, K1, K2 tog; slip sts from st holder (First Side) onto empty needle, with **wrong** side facing, slip 1 as if to **knit**, K1, PSSO, K1, P4, K3, P1: 20 sts.

Row 2: K1, P3, K4, P4, K4, P3, K1.

Row 3: P1, K3, P4, K4, P4, K3, P1.

Row 4: K1, M1, P3, work Back Cable, P4, work Front Cable, P3, M1, K1: 22 sts.

Row 5: P1, K4, (P4, K4) twice, P1.

Row 6: K1, P2, (work Back Twist, work Front Twist) twice, P2, K1.

Row 7: P1, K2, P2, K4, P4, K4, P2, K2, P1.

Row 8: K1, P2, K2, P4, work Front Cable, P4, K2, P2, K1.

Row 9: P1, K2, P2, K4, P4, K4, P2, K2, P1.

Row 10: K1, P2, K2, P4, K4, P4, K2, P2, K1.

Rows 11-13: Repeat Rows 7-9.

Row 14: K1, P2, (work Front Twist, work Back Twist) twice, P2, K1.

Row 15: P1, K4, (P4, K4) twice, P1.

Row 16: K1, P2 tog, P2, work Front Cable, P4, work Back Cable, P2, P2 tog, K1: 20 sts.

Row 17: P1, K3, P4, K4, P4, K3, P1.

Row 18: K1, P2 tog, P1, K2, work Front Twist, work Back Twist, K2, P1, P2 tog, K1: 18 sts.

Row 19: P1, K2, P2, K2, P4, K2, P2, K2, P1.

Row 20: K1, P2, K2, P2, work Front Cable, P2, K2, P2, K1.

Row 21: P1, K2, P2, K2, P4, K2, P2, K2, P1.

Row 22: K1, P2, K2, P2, K4, P2, K2, P2, K1.

Row 23: P1, K2, P2, K2, P4, K2, P2, K2, P1.

Row 24: K1, P2 tog, K2 tog, P2 tog, work Front Cable, P2 tog, K2 tog, P2 tog, K1: 12 sts.

Row 25: P2 tog across; cut yarn leaving a long end for sewing: 6 sts.

Thread yarn needle with end and slip remaining sts onto yarn needle; gather tightly and secure end.

SOLE
With larger size needles and leaving a long end for sewing, cast on 7{8-9} sts.

Row 1: Purl across.

Row 2 (Right side)**:** Increase in each st across: 14{16-18} sts.

Note: Loop a short piece of yarn around any stitch to mark Row 2 as **right** side and heel.

Row 3: P2, (K1, P1) across.

Row 4: K2, (P1, K1) across.

Repeat Rows 3 and 4 for Seed Stitch until Sole measures approximately 9{10-11}"/23{25.5-28} cm from cast on edge, ending by working Row 4.

Last Row: P2 tog across; cut yarn leaving a long end for sewing: 7{8-9} sts.

Thread yarn needle with end and slip remaining sts onto yarn needle; gather tightly and secure end.

Thread yarn needle with end at cast on edge. To form the heel, weave needle through cast on sts; gather tightly, allowing heel to cup, and secure yarn.

FINISHING
RIBBING
With smaller size needles and **right** sides facing, pick up 40{44-48} sts evenly spaced along end of rows at inside edge of Sides *(Fig. 18a, page 62)*.

Work in K1, P1 ribbing for 2" (5 cm).

Bind off all sts loosely leaving a long end for sewing.

Using a single strand of yarn, weave Ribbing and cast on edges of Sides together *(Fig. 19, page 63)*; sew Top to Sole.

Design by Cathy Hardy.

accessory clutch

Finished Size: 7" wide x 4" high
(18 cm x 10 cm)

MATERIALS

Medium Weight Yarn

[4 ounces, 203 yards
(113 grams, 186 meters) per skein]:
Solid - 1 skein
[3.5 ounces, 180 yards
(100 grams, 165 meters) per skein]:
Variegated - 1 skein
Straight knitting needles, size 7 (4.5 mm) **or**
size needed for gauge
Yarn needle
Sewing needle and matching thread
7" (18 cm) Zipper
Fabric for lining - 10" square

GAUGE: In Seed Stitch, 8 sts = 2" (10 cm)

Gauge Swatch: 2" (10 cm) wide
Cast on 8 sts.
Row 1: (K1, P1) across.
Row 2: (P1, K1) across.
Rows 3-8: Repeat Rows 1 and 2, 3 times.
Bind off all sts.

Techniques used:
- M1 *(Figs. 9a & b, page 61)*
- P2 tog *(Fig. 15, page 62)*
- SSP *(Fig. 17, page 62)*

STITCH GUIDE

FRONT CROSS (uses 2 sts)
Working in **front** of first st on left needle, knit into the second st making sure not to drop it off, then knit the first st letting both sts drop off the needle *(Figs. 4a & b, page 59)*.
BACK CROSS (uses 2 sts)
Working **behind** first st on left needle, knit into the **front** of second st making sure not to drop it off, then knit the first st letting both sts drop off the needle *(Figs. 5a & b, page 59)*.

BACK

The Back is worked in Seed Stitch with one edge stitch on each side that is worked in Stockinette Stitch for ease of assembly.

With Variegated yarn and leaving a long end for sewing, cast on 30 sts.

Row 1: P2, (K1, P1) across.

Row 2: K2, (P1, K1) across.

Repeat Rows 1 and 2 until Back measures approximately 4" (10 cm) from cast on edge, ending by working Row 1; do **not** cut yarn.

FRONT

Rows 1-3 (Turning ridge)**:** Knit across.

Row 4: P2, (K1, P1) across.

Row 5: K2, (P1, K1) across.

Row 6: P2, (K1, P1) across; cut yarn.

Row 7 (Right side - Increase row)**:** With Solid yarn, K5, M1, (K4, M1) 5 times, K5: 36 sts.

Row 8: P5, K1, (P4, K1) across to last 5 sts, P5.

Row 9: K5, P1, work Front Cross, work Back Cross, P1, ★ K4, P1, work Front Cross, work Back Cross, P1; repeat from ★ once **more**, K5.

Row 10: P5, K1, (P4, K1) across to last 5 sts, P5.

Row 11: K1, P5, work Back Cross, work Front Cross, ★ P6, work Back Cross, work Front Cross; repeat from ★ once **more**, P5, K1.

Repeat Rows 8-11 for pattern until Front measures approximately 3¼" (8.5 cm) from Turning ridge, ending by working Row 11.

TOP BORDER

Row 1 (Decrease row)**:** P5, SSP, P2, P2 tog, (P4, SSP, P2, P2 tog) twice, P5; cut yarn: 30 sts.

Row 2: With Variegated, knit across.

Row 3: P2, (K1, P1) across.

Row 4: K2, (P1, K1) across.

Rows 5 and 6: Repeat Rows 3 and 4.

Bind off all sts in pattern leaving last st on needle.

Strap: Add on 40 sts *(Figs. 6a & b, page 59)*.

Bind off all sts in **knit**; cut yarn leaving a long end for sewing.

FINISHING

Fold the Clutch in half at the Turning Ridge. Weave side seams *(Fig. 19, page 63)*; sew the end of the Strap to the same corner.

Make the lining to fit the Clutch, sewing the zipper to the opening.

Insert the lining into the Clutch and sew the top edge of the lining to the top edge of the Clutch.

Design by Cathy Hardy.

thank you for helping warm up america!

Since 1991, Warm Up America! has donated more than 250,000 afghans to battered women's shelters, victims of natural disaster, the homeless, and many others who are in need.

You can help Warm Up America! help others, and with so little effort. Debbie urges everyone who uses the patterns in this book to take a few minutes to knit a 7" x 9" (18 cm x 23 cm) block for this worthy cause. To help you get started, she's providing these two block patterns to knit.

If you are able to provide a completed afghan, Warm Up America! requests that you donate it directly to any charity or social services agency in your community.

Visit www.craftyarncouncil.com for more information.

MOSS ZIGZAG BLOCK
Multiple of 7 sts.

Cast on 28 sts.

Row 1 (Right side)**:** (P1, K1, P1, K4) across.

Row 2: (P4, K1, P1, K1) across.

Row 3: (K1, P1) twice, (K4, P1, K1, P1) across to last 3 sts, K3.

Row 4: P3, K1, P1, K1, (P4, K1, P1, K1) across to last st, P1.

Row 5: K2, P1, K1, P1, (K4, P1, K1, P1) across to last 2 sts, K2.

Row 6: P2, K1, P1, K1, (P4, K1, P1, K1) across to last 2 sts, P2.

Row 7: K3, P1, K1, P1, (K4, P1, K1, P1) across to last st, K1.

Row 8: (P1, K1) twice, (P4, K1, P1, K1) across to last 3 sts, P3.

Row 9: (K4, P1, K1, P1) across.

Row 10: (K1, P1, K1, P4) across.

Rows 11 and 12: Repeat Rows 7 and 8.

Rows 13 and 14: Repeat Rows 5 and 6.

Rows 15 and 16: Repeat Rows 3 and 4.

Repeat Rows 1-16 for pattern until Block measures approximately 9" (23 cm) from cast on edge.

Bind off all sts in pattern.

LITTLE SHELLS
Multiple of 7 sts + 2.

Techniques used:
- YO (*Figs. 8c & d, page 60*)
- P3 tog (*Fig. 16, page 62*)

Cast on 30 sts.

Row 1 (Right side)**:** Knit across.

Row 2: Purl across.

Row 3: K2, ★ YO, P1, P3 tog, P1, YO, K2; repeat from ★ across.

Row 4: Purl across.

Repeat Rows 1-4 for pattern until Block measures approximately 9" (23 cm) from cast on edge, ending by working a **wrong** side row.

Bind off all sts in **knit**.

general instructions

ABBREVIATIONS

cm	centimeters
K	knit
M1	make one
mm	millimeters
P	purl
PSSO	pass slipped stitch over
Rnd(s)	round(s)
SSK	slip, slip, knit
SSP	slip, slip, purl
st(s)	stitch(es)
tog	together
WYB	with yarn in back
WYF	with yarn in front
YO	yarn over

★ — work instructions following ★ as many **more** times as indicated in addition to the first time.

† to † — work all instructions from first † to second † **as many** times as specified.

( ) or [ ] — work enclosed instructions **as many** times as specified by the number immediately following **or** work all enclosed instructions in the stitch indicated **or** contains explanatory remarks.

colon (:) — the number given after a colon at the end of a row or round denotes the number of stitches you should have on that row or round.

work even — work without increasing or decreasing in the established pattern.

KNITTING NEEDLES		
UNITED STATES	ENGLISH U.K.	METRIC (mm)
0	13	2
1	12	2.25
2	11	2.75
3	10	3.25
4	9	3.5
5	8	3.75
6	7	4
7	6	4.5
8	5	5
9	4	5.5
10	3	6
10½	2	6.5
11	1	8
13	00	9
15	000	10
17	---	12.75

KNIT TERMINOLOGY		
UNITED STATES		INTERNATIONAL
gauge	=	tension
bind off	=	cast off
yarn over (YO)	=	yarn forward (yfwd) **or** yarn around needle (yrn)

BEGINNER	Projects for first-time knitters using basic knit and purl stitches. Minimal shaping.
EASY	Projects using basic stitches, repetitive stitch patterns, simple color changes, and simple shaping and finishing.
INTERMEDIATE	Projects with a variety of stitches, such as basic cables and lace, simple intarsia, double-pointed needles and knitting in the round needle techniques, mid-level shaping and finishing.
EXPERIENCED	Projects using advanced techniques and stitches, such as short rows, fair isle, more intricate intarsia, cables, lace patterns, and numerous color changes.

GAUGE

Exact gauge is **essential** for proper size. Before beginning your project, make a sample swatch in the yarn and needle specified in the individual instructions. After completing the swatch, measure it, counting your stitches and rows or rounds carefully. If your swatch is larger or smaller than specified, **make another, changing needle size to get the correct gauge**. Keep trying until you find the size needles that will give you the specified gauge. Once proper gauge is obtained, measure width of piece approximately every 3" (7.5 cm) to be sure gauge remains consistent.

MARKERS

As a convenience to you, we have used markers to mark the beginning of a round or to mark placement of increases and decreases. Place markers as instructed. You may use purchased markers or tie a length of contrasting color yarn around the needle. When you reach a marker, slip it from the left needle to the right needle; remove it when no longer needed. When using double pointed needles, a split-ring marker can be placed around the first stitch in the round to indicate the beginning of the round. Move it up at the end of each round.

ZEROS

To consolidate the length of an involved pattern, zeros are sometimes used so that all sizes can be combined. For example, knit 0{2-0-2} means that the first and third sizes would do nothing, and the second and fourth sizes would knit 2 sts.

Yarn Weight Symbol & Names	LACE 0	SUPER FINE 1	FINE 2	LIGHT 3	MEDIUM 4	BULKY 5	SUPER BULKY 6
Type of Yarns in Category	Fingering, size 10 crochet thread	Sock, Fingering, Baby	Sport, Baby	DK, Light Worsted	Worsted, Afghan, Aran	Chunky, Craft, Rug	Bulky, Roving
Knit Gauge Range* in Stockinette St to 4" (10 cm)	33-40** sts	27-32 sts	23-26 sts	21-24 sts	16-20 sts	12-15 sts	6-11 sts
Advised Needle Size Range	000-1	1 to 3	3 to 5	5 to 7	7 to 9	9 to 11	11 and larger

*GUIDELINES ONLY: The chart above reflects the most commonly used gauges and needle sizes for specific yarn categories.

** Lace weight yarns are usually knitted on larger needles to create lacy openwork patterns. Accordingly, a gauge range is difficult to determine. Always follow the gauge stated in your pattern.

USING A CIRCULAR NEEDLE

Cast on as many stitches as instructed. Untwist and straighten the stitches on the needle to be sure that the cast on ridge lays on the inside of the needle and never rolls around the needle. Hold the needle so that the ball of yarn is attached to the stitch closest to the **right** hand point. Working each round on the outside of the circle, with the **right** side of the knitting facing you, work across the stitches on the left hand point *(Fig. 2)*.

Check to be sure that the cast on edge has not twisted around the needle. If it has, it is impossible to untwist it. The only way to fix this is to rip it out and return to the cast on row.

Fig. 2

DOUBLE POINTED NEEDLES

The stitches are divided evenly between three *(Fig. 3a)* or four double pointed needles as specified in the individual pattern. Form a triangle or a square with the needles *(Figs. 3b & c)*.

Do **not** twist the cast on edge. With the remaining needle, work across the stitches on the first needle. You will now have an empty needle with which to work the stitches from the next needle. Work the first stitch of each needle firmly to prevent gaps. Continue working around without turning the work.

Fig. 3a

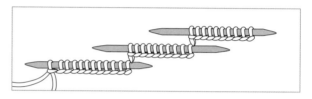

Fig. 3b

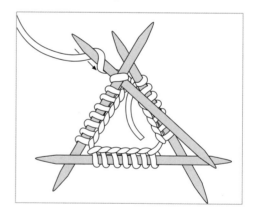

Fig. 3c

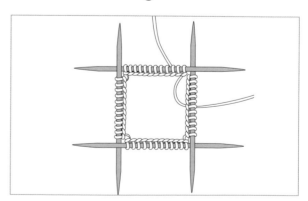

FRONT CROSS

Working in **front** of first stitch on left needle, knit into the second stitch making sure not to drop it off *(Fig. 4a)*, then knit the first stitch *(Fig. 4b)* letting both stitches drop off the needle.

Fig. 4a

Fig. 4b

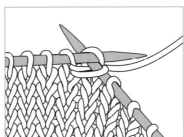

BACK CROSS

Working **behind** first stitch on left needle with yarn in back, knit into the **front** of second stitch *(Fig. 5a)* making sure **not** to drop it off, then knit the first stitch *(Fig. 5b)* letting both stitches drop off the needle.

Fig. 5a

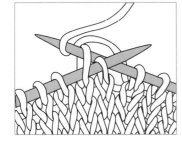

Fig. 5b

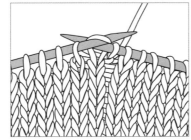

ADDING NEW STITCHES

Insert the right needle into the stitch as if to **knit**, yarn over and pull the loop through *(Fig. 6a)*, insert the left needle into the loop just worked from **front** to **back** and slip the loop onto the left needle *(Fig. 6b)*. Repeat for the required number of stitches.

Fig. 6a

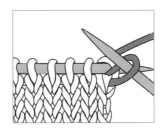

Fig. 6b

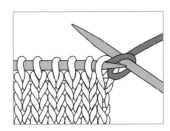

INCREASE

Knit the next stitch but do **not** slip the old stitch off the left needle *(Fig. 7a)*. Insert the right needle into the **back** loop of the **same** stitch and knit it *(Fig. 7b)*, then slip the old stitch off the left needle.

Fig. 7a

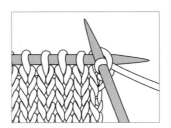

Fig. 7b

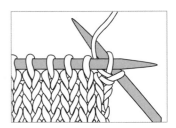

YARN OVERS *(abbreviated YO)*

A yarn over is simply placing the yarn over the right needle creating an extra stitch. Since the yarn over does produce a hole in the knit fabric, it is used for a lacy effect. On the row following a yarn over, you must be careful to keep it on the needle and treat it as a stitch by knitting or purling it as instructed.

To make a yarn over, you'll loop the yarn over the right needle like you would to knit or purl a stitch, bringing it either to the front or the back of the piece so that it'll be ready to work the next stitch, creating a new stitch on the needle as follows:

After a knit stitch, before a knit stitch
Bring the yarn forward **between** the needles, then back **over** the top of the right hand needle, so that it is now in position to knit the next stitch *(Fig. 8a)*.

Fig. 8a

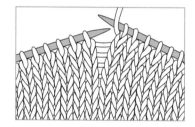

After a purl stitch, before a purl stitch
Take the yarn **over** the right hand needle to the back, then forward **under** it, so that it is now in position to purl the next stitch *(Fig. 8b)*.

Fig. 8b

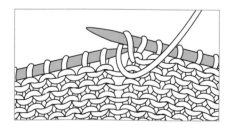

After a knit stitch, before a purl stitch
Bring the yarn forward **between** the needles, then back **over** the top of the right hand needle and forward **between** the needles again, so that it is now in position to purl the next stitch *(Fig. 8c)*.

Fig. 8c

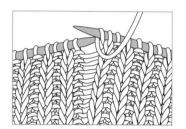

After a purl stitch, before a knit stitch
Take the yarn **over** the right hand needle to the back, so that it is now in position to knit the next stitch *(Fig. 8d)*.

Fig. 8d

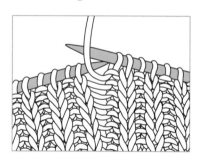

MAKE ONE *(abbreviated M1)*

Insert the **left** needle under the horizontal strand between the stitches from the **front** *(Fig. 9a)*, then knit into the **back** of the strand *(Fig. 9b)*.

Fig. 9a

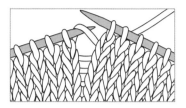

Fig. 9b

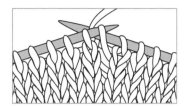

DECREASES

KNIT 2 TOGETHER *(abbreviated K2 tog)*

Insert the right needle into the **front** of the first two stitches on the left needle as if to **knit** *(Fig. 10)*, then **knit** them together as if they were one stitch.

Fig. 10

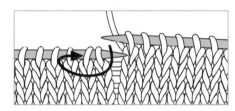

KNIT 3 TOGETHER *(abbreviated K3 tog)*

Insert the right needle into the **front** of the first three stitches on the left needle as if to **knit** *(Fig. 11)*, then **knit** them together as if they were one stitch.

Fig. 11

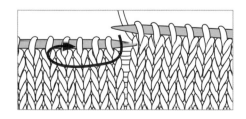

SLIP, SLIP, KNIT *(abbreviated SSK)*

Slip the first stitch as if to **knit**, then slip the next stitch as if to **knit** *(Fig. 12a)*. Insert the **left** needle into the **front** of both slipped stitches *(Fig. 12b)* and knit them together as if they were one stitch *(Fig. 12c)*.

Fig. 12a

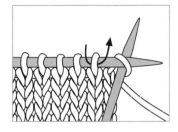

Fig. 12b

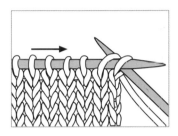

Fig. 12c

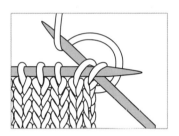

SLIP 1, KNIT 1, PASS SLIPPED STITCH OVER *(abbreviated slip 1, K1, PSSO)*

Slip one stitch as if to **knit** *(Fig. 13a)*. Knit the next stitch. With the left needle, bring the slipped stitch over the knit stitch just made *(Fig. 13b)* and off the needle.

Fig. 13a

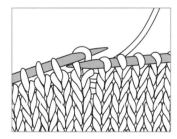

Fig. 13b

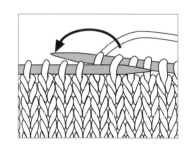

SLIP 1, KNIT 2, PASS SLIPPED STITCH OVER (abbreviated slip 1, K2, PSSO)

Slip one stitch as if to **knit** *(Fig. 13a, page 61)*. Knit the next two stitches. With the left needle, bring the slipped stitch over the two stitches just made *(Fig. 14)* and off the needle.

Fig. 14

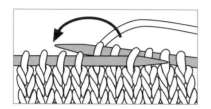

PURL 2 TOGETHER (abbreviated P2 tog)

Insert the right needle into the **front** of the first two stitches on the left needle as if to **purl** *(Fig. 15)*, then **purl** them together as if they were one stitch.

Fig. 15

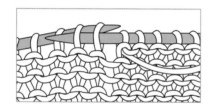

PURL 3 TOGETHER (abbreviated P3 tog)

Insert the right needle into the **front** of the first three stitches on the left needle as if to **purl** *(Fig. 16)*, then **purl** them together as if they were one stitch.

Fig. 16

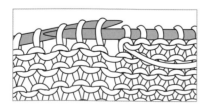

SLIP, SLIP, PURL (abbreviated SSP)

Slip the first stitch as if to **knit**, then slip the next stitch as if to **knit**. Place these two stitches back onto the left needle. Insert the **right** needle into the **back** of both slipped stitches from the **back** to **front** *(Fig. 17)* and purl them together as if they were one stitch.

Fig. 17

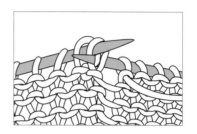

PICKING UP STITCHES

When instructed to pick up stitches, insert the needle from the **front** to the **back** under two strands at the edge of the worked piece *(Fig. 18a or b)*. Put the yarn around the needle as if to **knit**, then bring the needle with the yarn back through the stitch to the right side, resulting in a stitch on the needle.

Repeat this along the edge, picking up the required number of stitches.

A crochet hook may be helpful to pull yarn through.

Fig. 18a   Fig. 18b

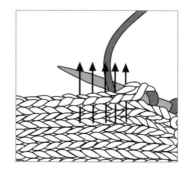
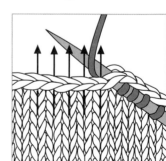

WEAVING SEAMS

With the **right** side of both pieces facing you and edges even, sew through both pieces once to secure the beginning of the seam, leaving an ample yarn end to weave in later. Insert the needle under the bar **between** the first and second stitches on the row and pull the yarn through *(Fig. 19)*. Insert the needle under the next bar on the second side. Repeat from side to side, being careful to match rows. If the edges are different lengths, it may be necessary to insert the needle under two bars at one edge.

Fig. 19

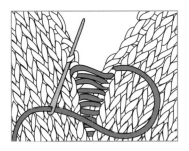

GRAFTING

Thread the yarn needle with the long end. Hold the threaded yarn needle on the right side of work.

Work in the following sequence, pulling yarn through as if to knit or as if to purl with even tension and keeping yarn under points of needles to avoid tangling and extra loops.

Step 1: Purl first stitch on **front** needle, leave on *(Fig. 20a)*.
Step 2: Knit first stitch on **back** needle, leave on *(Fig. 20b)*.
Step 3: Knit first stitch on **front** needle, slip off.
Step 4: Purl next stitch on **front** needle, leave on.
Step 5: Purl first stitch on **back** needle, slip off.
Step 6: Knit next stitch on **back** needle, leave on.
Repeat Steps 3-6 across until all stitches are worked off the needles.

Fig. 20a

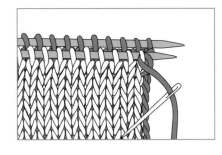

Fig. 20b

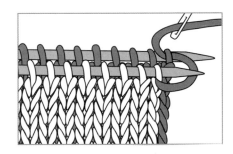

BLOCKING

Check the yarn label for any special instructions about blocking. With acrylics that can be blocked, place your project on a clean terry towel over a flat surface and pin in place to the desired size using rust-proof pins where needed. Cover it with dampened bath towels. When the towels are dry, the project is blocked.

Another method of blocking, that is especially good for wool, requires a steam iron or a handheld steamer. Place your project on a clean terry towel over a flat surface and shape to size; pin in place using rust-proof pins where needed. Hold a steam iron or steamer just above the item and steam it thoroughly. Never let the weight of the iron touch the item because it will flatten the stitches. Leave the item pinned until it is completely dry.

YARN INFORMATION

The projects in this book were made using a variety of yarns. Any brand in the specified weight may be used. It is best to refer to the yardage/meters when determining how many skeins or balls to purchase. Remember, to arrive at the finished size, it is the GAUGE/TENSION that is important, not the brand of yarn.

For your convenience, listed below are the specific yarns used to create our photography models.

BEADED WEDDING SET
Jade Sapphire Exotic Fibres, Mongolian Cashmere 2-ply
#000 Ivory

SPIRAL SOCKS
Universal Yarn® Debbie Macomber Blossom Street™ Collection, Petals Socks
#602 Alpine Strawberry

TEXTURED SHAWL
Universal Yarn® Debbie Macomber Blossom Street™ Collection, Rosebud
#501 Bleeding Heart

LACE SCARF
Patons® Lace
#33315 Sachet

SPA CLOTH & SOAP SACK
Bernat® Handicrafter® Cotton
#00030 Pale Yellow

BABY BONNET & BOOTIES SET
Bernat® Baby
Yellow - #21436 Yellow
White - #21402 White

RAINBOW FLOWERS BABY BLANKET
Bernat® Baby
White - #21402 White
Blue - #21451 Baby Blue
Purple - #21185 Soft Lilac
Yellow - #21436 Yellow
Pink - #21469 Pink

BALLS
Lily® Sugar'n Cream®
#01742 Hot Blue
#01712 Hot Green
#02743 Summer Splash

CABLE HAT & MITTENS
Universal Yarn® Debbie Macomber Blossom Street™ Collection, Cashmere Fleur De Lys
#407 Envy

COWL
Universal Yarn® Debbie Macomber Blossom Street™ Collection, Wild Meadow
#306 Juneau

CABLE SLIPPERS
Premier™ Yarns, Deborah Norville Collection, Everyday™ Soft Worsted
#ED100-10 Aubergine

ACCESSORY CLUTCH
Premier™ Yarns, Deborah Norville Collection, Everyday™ Soft Worsted
Solid - #ED100-07 Really Red
Variegated - #ED200-23 Red Rocks

WARM UP AMERICA BLOCKS
Lion Brand® Vanna's Choice®
#130 Honey
#158 Mustard

We have made every effort to ensure that these instructions are accurate and complete. We cannot, however, be responsible for human error, typographical mistakes, or variations in individual work. Instructions tested and photo models made by JoAnn Bowling, Nancy Desmarais, Lee Ellis, Raymelle Greening, and Dale Potter.